A Prayer Handbook
FOR DANCERS
A Guide to Supernatural Breakthrough in Spiritual Warfare

Everyday prayers for professional to non-professional dancers for those in theater, stage, television and film.

SWAZETTE WHITTEN

ISBN: 978-1-7364818-0-6 (Paperback)
ISBN: 978-1-7364818-1-3 (eBook)

Scriptures marked "KJV" are taken from the
King James Version of the Bible.

Copyright © 2020 Swazette Whitten.

All rights reserved. No part of this book may be reproduced, stored, or transmitted by any means—whether auditory, graphic, mechanical, or electronic—without written permission of both publisher and author, except in the case of brief excerpts used in critical articles and reviews. Unauthorized reproduction of any part of this work is illegal and is punishable by law.

Dedication

I would like to dedicate this book to the Father that I only knew, Daddy God. Father, you inspired me to write this book. You showed me that it can be done through the strength that you gave me. Also, what motivated me to write this book was the dancers that I met in my time of growing and still growing as a dancer. I met many dancers and through conversations regarding dance, it was revealed that intercession is needed, especially for those that struggle in the dance arena excelling to your purpose. This book is for those dancers who need intercessory prayer in the marketplace such as their professional dance careers; in a dance company, performing on Broadway, Television, and Media, having your dance studio or school. If you are in ministry such as traveling with your dance team or are part of a local dance ministry within their church, this is to encourage you! Don't give up and you can do it!!!! Keep your eyes on the promise.

I would like to acknowledge all of those that stood with me in prayer to the birth of this book.

I would like to acknowledge all the Intercessors for Praying For The Arts that prayed for me during the time I was writing this book. I would like to acknowledge Dr. Ellie for taking the time to proof read this manuscript for making sure it was sound in the Word of God. I would like to acknowledge Helena, for checking in on me to make sure that it was completed.

I would like to acknowledge my mother, Anna, for paying for my first dance lesson and introducing me to the gift of dance. I would like to acknowledge my dad, Roland, for the word says that the hearts of the fathers will be turned toward their children. I thank the Lord that I was able to build a relationship with my natural father. I thank you, Dad, for sowing into my life and paying for my theater classes.

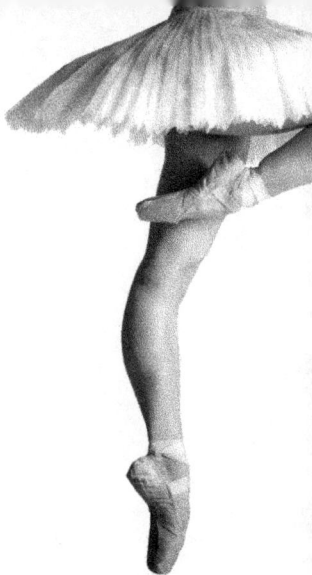

This book is written to the dancer, however, anyone in the performing arts industry can glean from this book.

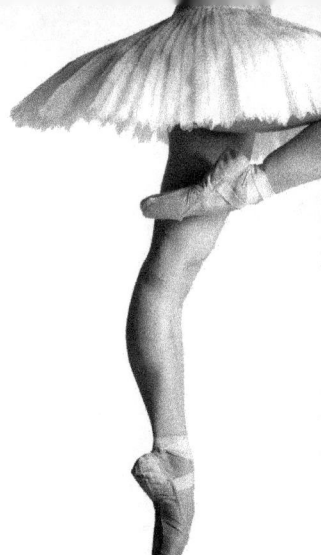

The Father God seeks those to worship Him. We must worship Him in spirit and in truth. Whether we are a non-professional to a professional dancer, we must realize where our talent comes from. In whatever capacity the Lord has called you to dance-dance as David did with all your might. Be a light to the saved and the unsaved. "Let your light so shine before men, that they may see your good works, and glorify your Father which is in heaven" (Matthew 5:16 KJV).

Prayer for dedicating your talent to the Lord

If you have not received Jesus Christ as your Lord and Savior, I would like to introduce to you, my friend and big brother. His name is Jesus. You will need the Lord to survive in the world of the Creative Arts. It only takes the strength of the Lord to walk in Holiness, Integrity, Righteousness, Honesty, and Accountability. He will teach you how to be a servant as well as a worshiper of Him. You will also need the gift of discernment as well, especially if the Lord has called you to dance professionally.

I would like to lead you into a prayer to receive Jesus Christ as Lord over your life. I want to explain the importance of this prayer. The bible says that if you confess the Lord Jesus Christ in your heart and believe that Jesus Christ was raised from the dead you will be saved. For the bible says in (Romans 10:9, 10) for with the heart you believe but with the mouth, confession is made unto salvation. Also, those who call upon the name of the Lord shall be saved.

The bible says that it is the will of the Father that no man should perish, but that all come to repentance. The prayer is this **(please pray this prayer out loud)**.

Father God, I believe that you sent your son Jesus Christ to die on the cross for my sins, and I believe that he rose on the third day. I ask that for your Holy Spirit to come to dwell in me and live inside of me this day. I dedicate my body, soul, mind, and spirit unto you in Jesus's name. I present my body a living sacrifice holy and acceptable unto you, which is your reasonable service. I choose this day to walk in the way that you would want me to go, in Jesus's name Amen. It is important that you read your bible every day. You have to feed your spirit man that is now born again. Let the Lord lead you where he would want you to go to church. It is also important that you surround yourself with Christian friends. The bible says he who makes himself friendly shall have a friend (Proverbs 18:24).

Dancers,

It is my prayer that through the gift of dance that you will embrace and walk in the gift of intercession. That as a worshiper of God, when you move in dance, the captives will be set free and yokes will be destroyed because of the power of God that resides in your spirit.

Table of Contents

I. Everyday Prayers for Dancers

1. Prayer for Protection for Limbs and Bones......... 1
2. Prayer for Creativity 3
3. Prayer Against the Spirit of Envy and Jealousy.. 7
4. Prayer for Your Ministry 9
5. Prayer for Repentance 11
6. Prayer for Backslidden Dancers........................... 13
7. Prayer against Sexual Sin...................................... 15
8. Prayer for Teachers 19
9. Prayer for Students 23
10. Prayer for Parents 27
11. Prayer for your Church 31
12. Prayer for your Pastor 33
13. Prayer for Your Government Leaders................ 35

II. Prayers for the Professional Dancer

1. Prayers for going on Auditions 41
2. Rejection From Auditions 43
3. Prayer for Directors, Actors, and Production Staff 45
4. Prayer for Your Dance Company 47
5. Prayer for A Dance Company 51
6. Prayer for Tithing on Your Performing Arts Business 53
7. Prayer for a Building 57
8. Prayer for a New Building 59
9. Prayer for Choreography 61
10. Prayer for More Students 63
11. Prayer Against Plagiarism and Protecting Your Work 65

III. Prayers for the Pre-Professional and Non-Professional Dancer

1. Prayer for a Healthy Diet 69
2. Prayer for Spiritual Growth 71
3. Prayer Against the Spirit of Fear 73
4. Prayer For Your Teacher 75
5. Prayer For Your Dance Team 77

IV. Prayers for Deliverance

1. Prayers Against the Spirit of Perversion 81
2. Removing Every Altar of Idolatry 85

I
Everyday Prayers for Dancers

Prayer For Salvation

Dear Heavenly Father, I come to you in Jesus's Name asking you to forgive me for my sins and to cleanse me from all unrighteousness. Lord, your word says that "for all have sinned, and come short of the glory of God" (Romans 3:23) and "none is righteous, no, not one" (Romans 3:11). I thank you, Lord, that through your son's death, Jesus Christ gave me the opportunity to become righteous. Your word says, "If we confess our sins, he is faithful and just to forgive us our sins, and to cleanse us from all unrighteousness" (1 John 1:9). Therefore, I renounce every tie with the world and every relationship that would hinder my growth in you. I believe that you sent your son Jesus Christ to die on the cross for my sins and that He rose on the third day. Because your Word says, "That if thou shalt confess with thy mouth the Lord Jesus, and shalt believe in thine heart that God hath raised him from the dead, thou shalt be saved." For with the heart, man believeth unto righteousness; and with the mouth, confession is made unto salvation" (Romans 10: 9, 10). Therefore, I confess and believe in my heart that Christ has risen from the dead and that I will be saved. I ask that your Holy Spirit now make its home in me in Jesus's name, Amen.

Reference Scriptures: (Romans 3:23; Romans 3:11; 1 John 1: 9; Romans 10: 9, 10 KJV).

1

Prayer for Protection for Limbs and Bones

The Blood, The Blood, The Blood, The Blood of Jesus over my body right now in the powerful name of Jesus Christ of Nazareth. Father God, right now in Jesus's name, I cover my organs, vessels, my limbs, and my bones with the blood of Jesus Christ of Nazareth, and I pray for a hedge of protection around me and my limbs and bones. Father God, I ask that you would give me the wisdom to warm up my muscles and not rush to start any rehearsal, ministering or performance. Lord, I ask that I will have a conscious effort to do the right thing concerning protecting my limbs and bones in Jesus's Name. I come against any mishaps in rehearsals, ministering, and performance. I ask that you would give me wisdom in how to move my body that I would not "over-step" or misjudge a move that would cause injury to me in the name of Jesus. I bind the spirit of envy, jealousy, and the "evil-eye" against my stature, my movement, my flexibility, my technique, and my worship and adoration to you. Any arrows and fiery darts that the enemy sends my way, I send them back to the enemy's camp in Jesus's Name. Let God arise and let every enemy be scattered (Psalm 68:1)! Be scattered off of my worship and praise to you, be scattered off of my technique, be scattered off of my gifts and anointing!!! Father God, Your Word says that *"He keepeth all his bones and not one of them is broken"* (Psalm 34:20). Your Word also says, *"A bone of him shall not be broken"* (John 19:36). I thank you, Lord, that my body, limbs, and bones are covered under the blood of Jesus Christ, in Jesus Name, Amen.

Reference Scriptures: (Psalm 68:1; Psalm 34:20; John 19:36 KJV).

2

Prayer for Creativity

Dancers, this is a prayer for creativity. Whatever you feel you need the Lord's help in your assignment, he will bless you and increase your wisdom and allow creativity to flow through you.

Father God, you are the God of Creativity. There is none like you. You created the heavens and earth in six days and rested on the seventh day. You also created man in your image and in your likeness. Therefore, I ask that you stir up the gift of creativity within me. I ask that my thoughts will be aligned with your thoughts to create _____. Holy Spirit, move on my behalf. Let me have dreams and visions of this task. Give me godly instruction, even as you gave instructions to Noah to create and build the ark. I ask that you will anoint my spiritual eyes and ears so that I can see and hear your instructions. Even in areas I lack wisdom, I ask that you send godly helpers to bring forth this _____ to help put it in motion. Your Word also says, *"If any of you lack wisdom, let him ask of God, that giveth to all men liberally, and upbraideth not; and it shall be given him"* (James 1:5). Father, I ask that you will give me wisdom and understanding to walk in my creativity. Father, you gave Daniel a discerning spirit to walk in wisdom and to be ten times better than the Babylonian children (Daniel 1:20). I, therefore, ask that your hand will be on this _____ project that it will bring you glory. I bind every demon spirit that has affected my creative gifts from coming forth. Father, your word says whatever I bind on earth shall be bound in heaven. Whatever I loose on earth shall be loosed in heaven (Matthew 18:18). Let every dormant gift of creativity come forth. I command every dormant gift that is programmed in my DNA to come forth. I command it to arise right now in Jesus's Name. Father God, your Word says to call those things that be not as though they were. I thank you, Lord, that I am walking in your divine grace, anointing and elevation to bring your vision to pass through my gift of creativity. I thank you, Lord, for specific creative instructions for this project. I thank you, Lord, that this project will be completed by your ordained calendar. I thank you, Lord, for the gift of creativity and wisdom along with understanding. I thank you for the success of this project, in Jesus's Name Amen.

Reference Scriptures: (Daniel 1: 20; Genesis 1; Genesis 2: 1-3; Genesis 6: 14-22; James 1:5; Romans 4:17b, KJV).

3

Prayer Against the Spirit of Envy and Jealousy

Father God, right now in Jesus's Name, I repent for coveting _____'s gift in dance and I ask that you would remove anything in my heart toward him/her that would cause me to have an envious or jealous spirit. I tear down any altar in my heart of envy and jealousy, and I replace it with praise for you and the gifts that you have given me. I ask that you would bless _____ for his/her anointing and gifts. I ask that you increase them and let your glory be seen through them when they dance. Now, Lord, I cover my heart with the Blood of Jesus, I ask that you remove every altar that has been made in my heart that would cause me to be envious or jealous in Jesus's Name. I ask that your glory will be seen through me, through my actions, my attitudes, and when I dance. I thank you, Lord, that I shall not lack or want for anything concerning my gifts and calling in dance. I thank you, Lord, that your Word says, *"For he that cometh to God must believe that he is, and that he is a rewarder of them that diligently seek him"* (Hebrews 11:6, KJV). I thank you, Lord, that when the tempter comes that he will not find anything in me that represents him, in Jesus's Name Amen.

Reference Scriptures: (Matthew 4:3; 2 Corinthians 4:6; Psalm 34:10; Hebrews 11:6).

Prayer for Your Ministry

As dancers, you are considered part of the Levitical Priesthood. The Levitical Priesthood is from the tribe of Levi and is those that are called to minister unto the Lord. Therefore, you and your ministry have to walk in holiness. For the word says, "for I am the Lord that bringeth you up out of the land of Egypt, to be your God: ye shall therefore be holy, for I am holy" (Leviticus 11:45 KJV) and "because it is written, Be ye holy, for I am holy" (1 Peter 1:16 KJV). So, dance ministers, we have to walk in holiness. We cannot do what we see others do because we are called to a higher calling. Whatever we do, we are held to higher accountability as we can make someone stumble in his or her walk with Christ.

So, Father God, right now I come to you in Jesus's name, I pray over my ministry's foundation. Anything that has been planted that does not align itself in holiness I command it to be uprooted right now in Jesus's name. I ask that you would expose any error that this ministry is walking in, any error that I am walking in, or any leader in this ministry. I break every assignment that has been sent over this ministry to not walk in a holy lifestyle. Father God, I ask that you purge and purify this ministry and the members that are attached to this ministry. I pray that this ministry will be rooted and grounded in the Word of God and that we will be led by the Holy Spirit. I pray that we will have a heart to minister your Word through the arts and that you will get the glory. Father, right now in Jesus's name, I re-dedicate my ministry to you. I ask that you be Lord over this ministry and that you will direct me in every decision that I make. I ask that you and your Word will be the final decision maker in this ministry. Let not the foot of pride come upon the members of this ministry and me. I ask you, Lord, to have your way. Let your Kingdom come, and your will be done on earth as it is in Heaven, In Jesus's name, Amen.

Reference Scriptures: (Leviticus 11:45; 1 Peter 1:16).

5

Prayer for Repentance

Father, your word says if my people who are called by my name shall humble themselves and pray and seek my face and turn from their wicked ways, then I will hear from heaven and forgive their sin and heal their land. Lord, I repent for _____. I confess my sin before you. You are faithful and just to forgive me of my sin and to cleanse me from all unrighteousness. Wash me with your son's blood. Create in me a clean heart, and renew a right spirit within me, strengthen me to never to return to this situation or problem again. Help me, Lord, to renew my mind daily in your word for this particular situation. And now Lord I renounce all part of _____ and never to go back to it. Help me to guard my heart. I pray for your wisdom in this area in Jesus's name. Amen.

Reference Scriptures: (2 Chronicles 7:14, I John 1:9, Psalm 51)

6

Prayer for Backslidden Dancers

Lord God, your word says that you are married to the backslider (Jeremiah 3:14). I thank you, Lord, even as in the book of Hosea, when the children of Israel were backslidden, you still loved them. Now, Lord, your word says, *"If my people which are called by my name, shall humble themselves, and pray, and seek my face, and turn from their wicked ways, then will I hear from heaven, and will forgive their sin, and will heal their land"* (2 Chronicles 7:14). I thank you, Lord, for this day, I humble myself, and I turn from the lust of the eyes the lust of the flesh and the pride of life. Because your word says love not the world neither anything that's in the world (1 John 2:15). I renounce my love for anything that drew me away from you. Father, I ask that you will give me a new heart, a heart that is after your ways. I close the door to my past now and my former life. I give you full permission to remove anything or anyone from my path that would cause me to backslide. Any unholy habits I ask that you show me in Jesus name. And right now, I take authority over everything that is not of you. I bind every spirit that would cause me to backslide right now in Jesus's name. Father, even the path that I walk, whether it's going to work, school, or church, Lord, if this pathway would bring people that would harm me, I ask that you would turn my feet around in Jesus's name. Give me wisdom in how to travel to my destination and allow those that would try to harm me or lead me into sin not to see me. Lord, I now ask that you show me how to renew my mind in your word concerning this area. I pray for godly friends in Jesus's name. I close the door to my past and former relationships, and I no longer open it. Any curse that came on my life through my disobedience I break its power right now in Jesus name. I thank you, Lord, for healing my land, and I thank you for the victory in Jesus's name, Amen.

Reference Scriptures: (Jeremiah 3: 14; 2 Chronicles 7:14; 1 John 2:15 KJV)

7

Prayer against Sexual Sin

Dear Dancers,

The sin that would hurt the Father the most is sexual sin. Our bodies are the temple of the Holy Spirit, and the devil will try to defile you in any way, whether it's having illegal sex (sex without being married) or masturbation. God calls us to walk in holiness. For his word says to be holy for he is holy. If you are struggling in this area, I suggest that you seek deliverance and counseling from your local church. Also, if you continue to crucify your flesh of fleshly appetites, the Lord will help you in this area. I also suggest that you do a lot of fasting and praying and to stop all contact from any parties that would get you to fall in these areas.

Please list the names of all the parties that you had sexual encounters with and put their names in the proper place. The bible says, "that if we confess our sins He is faithful and just to forgive us and to cleanse us from all unrighteousness" (1 John 1: 9).

Lord, it is your desire for us to worship you in spirit and in truth (John 4:23, 24). Lord, right now I dedicate my body unto you as a living sacrifice holy, acceptable which is your reasonable service. Father God, your word says, *"If we confess our sins, he is faithful and just to forgive us our sins, and to cleanse us from all unrighteousness"* (1 John 1:9). Father God, you called me to walk in holiness, so right now I repent for opening the door to sexual sin, and I ask that you forgive me in Jesus's name. I repent for any sexual contact with (please list names) _____ and I ask that you forgive me, and I forgive myself. I break soul-ties with (please list names) _____ and I close the door to sexual sin with (please list names) _____ right now in Jesus's name. Any demon spirit that has been associated with this relationship, I command you to go right now, in Jesus's name. Father God, I ask that you restore my soul and in any area of my life that this person has affected. Father God, you said in your word that if I live after the flesh that it shall bring spiritual death (Romans 8:12, 13). Therefore, I choose to put to death the things that will further me away from you. Lord, right now, I rededicate my spirit, soul, and body to you. Father God, I make a conscious effort to be renewed in the spirit in my mind in this area and will no longer give the devil any room. Lord God, I ask that you fill me in any area of my life where I lack that you may be glorified, In Jesus's name, Amen.

Reference Scriptures: John 4:23, 24; 1 John 1:9; Romans 8:12, 13; Romans 12:1, 2; Ephesians 4:22-24.

8

Prayer for Teachers

Father God, your Word says to guard my heart with all diligence, for out of it flows the issues of life. So Father God, right now in Jesus's name, I ask that you purge out of my heart anything that is not of you. Every spiritual altar that exalts itself against the knowledge of God in my heart, I tear it down right now in Jesus's name. Lord, you said whatsoever I bind on earth shall be bound in heaven and whatsoever I loose on earth shall be loose in heaven. I bind the altar of self, people-pleasing, backbiting, and gossiping with dancers, dance moms, or anyone else. Lord, I ask that you will bridle my tongue and that I will not partake of anything that will defile my spirit. Lord, I pray for those that I have hurt through my tongue or actions. I ask that you forgive me for hurting and offending them. I pray that you will bless _____ and that you will heal them of any hurt that I may have caused them. Now Lord, the enemy is trying to bring division and un-forgiveness with _____ and myself. So, therefore, I bind the spirit of un-forgiveness that is attacking their mind. I ask that they will be loose from any thoughts of un-forgiveness toward me. I pray that you will continue to work on them as you are working on me.

Father, in the name of Jesus, any person that the enemy will try to use as a distraction to get me off focus from my assignment, I come against the spirit operating behind them in Jesus name. I ask that they will be focused on their God-given assignments in Jesus's name.

So, Father, I pray for this leadership position that you put me in. I pray that I will not walk in pride, the lust of the eyes, and the lust of the flesh. I pray for each day that you would give me wisdom and revelation knowledge in my authority and spiritual and natural gifts. I pray for the eyes of my understanding to be enlightened that I will know the hope of my calling. I pray that you will give me revelation knowledge every day on how I can advance your kingdom through my gift of dance.

I ask that as you enlarge my territory that I will not become boastful or proud. I also ask that when you bring new people to be a part of new assignments that I will be able to discern their gifts, talents, abilities, and motives.

I also ask that you help me to know the faithful ones that have been a part of the ministry/dance company who you would want me to promote. Help me to discern people's motives. Help me to know who is for me and not for me. I ask that you increase my spiritual hearing that I may hear things that people may not hear. I ask that you increase my spiritual vision that I may see things that people may not want me to see. I ask that as you increase these abilities that I will conduct myself accordingly with employees, dancers, business relationships, spiritual leaders, politicians, and those that are producers and directors. Give me the wisdom to know when to speak and when not to speak. Let me be led by your spirit that you will direct my path. I ask that you will anoint my head with oil and let my cup run over with the blessings that you have for me and those associated with me in Jesus's name. Amen.

Reference Scriptures: (Proverbs 4:23; Matthew 18:18; Ephesians 1:17, 18; 1 Chronicles 4:10; Proverbs 3:6; Psalm 23: 5 KVJ).

9

Prayer for Students

Dear Students of the Creative Arts,

The reason why I address you as "students of the creative arts" is because you have more than the gift of dance that dwells in you. You may have the gift of song, acting, playwriting, etc. As a vessel unto the Lord, it is your responsibility that you continually keep your heart pure and your gifts pure. Do not let the enemy tempt you with things that may defile your gifts. As you grow in your relationship with God, the Holy Spirit will let you know what things you should partake of in the arts. You want God to use you mightily whether you are planning to dance on Broadway, Hollywood, Television, Media, or even in a professional dance company, you do not want to compromise your gifts. Remember, God has anointed and appointed you in this industry. Pray for your walk-in Him to be strong and committed. As you shine your light it will shine unto others to see that God will get the glory and your light will lead others to Christ. (Please pray the following prayer out loud).

Father God, I thank you for all the talents and abilities that you have given me. I dedicate them to you, and I ask that you help me be a good steward over each gift. Lord, your Word says that you have not given me a spirit of fear but of power, love, and of a sound mind. So, Lord, I ask that you would help me to walk in faith and help me to be disciplined in my season of learning dance. I ask that I will have a humble heart and that I will have a teachable spirit. Father God, help me to learn from those that I may find intolerable in the arts, but you have gifted them mightily. Help me to fully walk out your divine timetable over my life. Give me the wisdom to know who my mentors and teachers are that will help me in my time of growth. Help me not to miss any divine appointments with mentors, producers, directors, dance teachers, and others that you may have assigned to me or work on special projects. As I am blessed financially because of my talents, help me to be a good steward in giving my tithes and offerings to you. Help me to be faithful over my finances so that you will make me ruler over more financial blessings. Help me to be anxious for nothing but with prayer and supplication, let me continually uplift every step I take in you. I ask that you will order my steps. I thank you, Lord, for your divine timing, and I will continue to be led by your spirit. I thank you, Lord, for the victory in Jesus's name. Amen.

Reference Scriptures: (2 Timothy 1:7; Philippians 4:6; Psalm 37:23).

10

Prayer for Parents

Dear Parents,

Children are a blessing from God. God has entrusted you with those who are future leaders in various fields. It is a parent's responsibility to pray for their children and to help guide them in the right direction of their destiny. This responsibility is not easy, as you will have many life distractions that may try to hinder you from spending time in prayer for your children. Even as you are committed to seeing the gift of dance in your child mature, ask God daily to give you wisdom on how to pray. God may use your child to touch the nations with their creative gifts, and you do not want the enemy to steal their destiny. Ask God to fill your mouth daily with the right words on how to specifically pray for your child's creative talents and destiny. You are the prayer warrior for your child, and the heavens will move on your behalf as you stand in the gap and pray. Be bold with your prayers and make declarations and proclamations of faith for the future of your children. If you know that the Lord has called your child to greatness with their creative gifts, intercede for them to see the manifestation of the promises of God. On another note, pray for God to strengthen you as you continue to labor in prayer for your children. Additionally, God will give your sons and daughters mentors to help them cultivate and develop their creative gifts in the Arts. Pray for the right people to impart into their lives. Ask God to show you spiritually who their mentors are to help them before they may even manifest in the natural. Finally, as God begins to manifest His glory on your child's talents and abilities it will provoke jealousy from other children and parents. Do not be discouraged. Continue to press forward and make sure that you stand with a pure heart unto the Lord so that he will continue to hear and answer your prayers.

Father God, I come boldly before your throne of grace, and I ask that you forgive me of my sins knowingly and unknowingly. I stand in the gap and pray for my son/daughter _____. I ask that you give me wisdom on what and how to pray. I thank you, Lord, that as _____ was being formed in my womb, you ordained them to walk in their calling in the creative arts. I thank you Father for blessing me with my son/daughter _____. Help me to be faithful in prayer so that my son/daughter _____ will walk in the fullness of their calling in the creative talents. Now, Father, your Word says that if you are faithful over a few things that you will make us ruler over many. So Lord, as they are being shown faithful, let them maintain their integrity and not give in to malicious gossip, backbiting, jealousy, and envy. Help them to love those that persecute them because they are excelling in their God-given talents. I ask that you will keep _____ focused on their God-given assignment. Let them continually show love to anyone who may have any malice toward them. Father God, right now, I bind the spirit of jealousy and envy against my son/daughter _____ that they will bear much fruit in their gifts. I ask that you will enlarge their territory and bless them that they will be a blessing to the world and the nations. I pray for other children that they may dance with; I ask that you will bless them as well. May they be fruitful in their talents and their abilities. I ask that you will show their parents how to pray for their children as well. I thank you, Lord. Lord your Word says how good and pleasant it is for us to walk in unity. I thank you, Lord that as my child and other children are working together on dance projects that they are walking together in unity. I thank you, Lord, for the manifestation of my prayers, and the fruit shall remain in Jesus's name. Amen.

Reference Scriptures: (Matthew 25:23; 1 Chronicles 4:10; Psalm 133:1).

11

Prayer for your Church

Father God, right now in Jesus's name, I pray for my local assembly. I pray for a hedge of protection around them. I pray that they will walk in the spirit of favor and that they will constantly seek the Lord's counsel in their daily activities. I pray that they will walk in unity and in love with their loved ones and their brothers and sisters in the Lord. I pray that they will have a hunger and a thirst after righteousness; I pray that you will bless the work of their hands and that you may give them the spirit of wisdom and revelation so that they may know who they are in you and that no devil in hell can deceive them from their calling and destiny. I pray, Father God, that their heart will be enlightened that they will know the hope of their calling.

Reference Scripture: (Ephesians 1: 17, 18).

12

Prayer for your Pastor

Father God, I uplift the man that you have called to watch over my soul. Father God, I pray that you would protect him/her from danger or harm. I pray that you would give them wisdom concerning every affair with ministry matters and personal matters. I pray for a hedge of protection around him/her and their family. Father God, I pray that you will meet every need above and beyond that they could possibly imagine or think according to the power that works in them. I pray for witty inventions. I pray for new dimensions in ministry for them. I pray that you will continually give them a new vision for the ministry. I come against any assassination for the man or woman of God in Jesus name. I bind every spirit of jealousy and envy over the ministry and I pray that you would continually bless the ministry, in Jesus's name, Amen.

13

Prayer for Your Government Leaders

Dear Dancers,

As the Levitical priesthood, it is expected of you to pray for your government leaders. The decisions that they make can ultimately affect things surrounding us. We should pray for our government leaders on a daily basis and ask God to lead them in their decision-making process. They are the ones that create policies; laws that will affect our generation and generations to come. Pray that those that are in office will do the will of our Heavenly Father and that they receive godly-counsel.

Father God, your word says, "I exhort therefore, that, first of all, supplications, prayers, intercessions, and giving of thanks, be made for all men; for kings, and for all that are in authority; that we may lead a quiet and peaceable life in all godliness and honesty" (1 Timothy 2:1, 2 KJV). So Lord, right now in Jesus's name, I stand in the gap for my government leaders. I ask that you will help them in their decision-making process and that when they are making decisions, they are being led by your spirit and godly-counsel. Father, I come against indecisiveness and the works of the flesh when they are making decisions. Let them see the plan and will of God concerning every decision they make. I bind the spirit of deception that the enemy will try to bring to them. Expose those that mean them no good who would try to hinder the will of God. I ask you, Father, right now, let every decision they make have a positive impact in the performing arts industry. I pray for governmental funds to flow into the performing arts. I pray for new grants to come forth, existing grants to be renewed, I pray for endowments in the arts. In particular, I pray that there will be much support in Christian works in Education, Broadway, Television, Movies, Media, Technology, and any other spheres of influence that you have ordained. I pray for the spirit of favor to rest upon those that you have called to be a creative artist and that they would get continual favor. Even as you anointed King Cyrus to give the children of Israel favor and to open the gates, and the gates shall not be shut. Now, Lord, I thank you for using government leaders to enlarge our territory so that we will be able to perform your divine will on this earth. I ask that you will bless those in authority. I pray for a hedge of protection around them and their families. I pray that when they bless your people that you will pour out your spirit upon them and that they will be blessed. Father, even as you have enlarged our territory, let us have wisdom on what to do when the increase pours into our hands. I ask that we will walk in your timing and not miss any opportunities that you would have for us. I thank you for opening doors that no man can open and closing doors that no man can close. I thank you for your miraculous power working on your children's behalf in Jesus's name. Amen.

Reference Scriptures: (Isaiah 61:6; Isaiah 45:1; 1 Peter 2: 9; Revelation 1: 4-6; 1 Timothy 2:1, 2; Revelation 3:8, Deuteronomy 12:3; Galatians 3:14).

II

Prayers for the Professional Dancer

Prayers for going on Auditions

Father God, your word says that the kings' heart is in your hand. Father God, I ask for the spirit of favor and wisdom to overtake me while I am preparing for auditions in Jesus's name. Lord God, I thank you for opening doors that no man can open. I thank you for revealing to me where my wealth is concerning every door that you are going to open for me, in Jesus's name. I thank you for divine favor. Let my audition tape stand out, and my choreography stand out, in Jesus's name. Father God, I thank you, Lord, for wisdom and a preparation strategy in preparing for this audition. I bind every spirit that would hinder me from going forth and being cast in the role right now in Jesus's name. I pray Lord, that my name would be chosen from among the many that came to audition. Father God, I ask that you enlarge my borders and my territory for being cast in a role that I can't possibly imagine or think according to the power that works in me. I thank you, Lord, for revelation knowledge continually, Jesus name. Amen!

2

Rejection From Auditions

Even the Almighty Heavenly Father had suffered rejection.

The children of Israel rejected God when they did not want Him to reign over them, but instead, they wanted a natural king. (I Samuel 8:7).

I thank you, Father God, that your love is endless. I thank you, Lord, that even as one door closes that you have another door ready to open that no man can shut. I thank you, Lord, that no weapon formed against me shall prosper. I thank you, Lord, no weapon against my emotions, my well-being, and even my destiny. And now Lord, you said in your word whatsoever I shall bind on earth shall be bound in heaven whatsoever I loose on earth shall be loosed in heaven. I bind the spirit of rejection off my life. I lose your divine favor. Lord, I pray, and I speak doors to open and to manifest in my life. I pray over my divine calendar that you have established in the Heavenlies. I pray that according to your will and plan that I will go through every door that you ordained for me to go through in Jesus name. I speak healing over my spirit man that the Almighty God loves me with an everlasting love. I thank you, Lord, that there is no depth, nor height that can separate me from your love. I thank you, Lord, for showering me with your love. And now, Lord, even as you would lead me to go back on another audition, give me your divine wisdom on how to prepare. I ask you, Lord, to put people in my path to show me how to prepare for where you would have me to go, in Jesus's name Amen.

Reference Scriptures: (Matthew 18:18, Revelation 3:8, Isaiah 54:17, Romans 8:39).

3

Prayer for Directors, Actors, and Production Staff

Father God, right now, in Jesus's name, I uplift the directors, actors, and production staff members. I cover them with the Blood of Jesus. I pray that we will work together in unity. Father, your Word says, "How good and how pleasant it is for brethren to dwell together in unity. It is like the precious ointment upon the head, that ran down upon the beard, even Aaron's beard: that went down to the skirts of his garments" (Psalm 133:1-2 KJV). I bind the spirit of strife and contention right now in Jesus name. Father your word says "whatever we bind on earth shall bind in heaven and whatever we lose on earth shall be lose in heaven. I lose the spirit of unity and peace over _____. I pray that you will guide their efforts and help them know how to handle their God-given responsibilities. I bless them, Lord. I ask that you will give them peace right now in Jesus's Name. I pray that you increase them right now in Jesus's name. Now Lord, I ask that you would remove any stumbling block in my relationship with _____ in Jesus's name.

Reference Scriptures: (Psalm 133:1-2, Mathew 18:18).

4

Prayer for Your Dance Company

Father God, right now in Jesus's name I come before you, asking for your divine wisdom in the direction of my dance company_____. I pray that every dancer will grow in their specific gifting and that they will not be lifted up with a spirit of pride. I come against the spirit of competition, strife, envy, and jealousy within the dance company. Father, your Word says, "*how good and how pleasant it is for brethren to dwell together in unity. It is like the precious ointment upon the head, that ran down upon the beard, even Aaron's beard: that went down to the skirts of his garments*" (Psalm 133:1, 2). I pray for the spirit of unity to operate fully in this company (Romans 15: 5, 6). I ask that when we dance together, on stage, that we will flow together like different instruments put together to make beautiful music for your glory. I pray that when we dance that we will make intercession with our movements and that shackles and chains will be broken off people, and they will be set free. I also ask that as the leader of _____, that I would continually submit to your divine will and authority. Father, your word says that if you are lifted up all men will be drawn unto you (John 12:31). So, therefore, Lord, I bind the spirit of pride or any other spirit that would try to glorify itself. I decree and declare that your name will be glorified in every decision concerning _____. I pray that you will give me the wisdom to know what assignments to take and what assignments to refuse. I pray that you will close every door that is not of you and that every door that is of you will remain open. Father, as we go forth I pray that this _____ dance company will operate in its divine fullness. I speak over the destiny of this company, and I speak greatness, I speak life, I speak the ability to operate in greater creativity that has not been seen on this earth. Father, your word says that now unto him who is able to do exceedingly, abundantly above all that we can ask or think according to the power that works in us (Ephesians 3:17-20). I thank you for your power works and reigns in us. I thank you for your divine direction and that we will fulfill our assignment here on this earth.

Now Lord, as we go before judges or panels of evaluators, I ask for your divine favor. I ask that we would be the head and not the tail that we would be above and not beneath (Deuteronomy 28:13). I pray that you would put in our spirit how to prepare for each production and each competition. I thank you, Lord, that you will be magnified in all we do, in Jesus's name I pray, Amen.

Reference Scriptures: (Psalm 133: 1, 2; Romans 15: 5,6; Ephesians 3:17-20, Deuteronomy 28:13).

5

Prayer for A Dance Company

Father, I thank you for the opportunity to be a part of _____ Dance Company. I thank you that many doors will open for _____ Dance Company. Now Lord, as we go forth in rehearsals and performances, I ask for your divine impartation on each dancer. I ask for your ability to operate on our ability and that you will get the glory in Jesus's name. I pray for the director and that he/she would be obedient to your call. I ask that they would set their face like a flint and that they will not be moved by the circumstances in the natural, but they will operate in the spirit realm. I pray for unity within the company. I pray that there would be no spirit of competition between us and that we will flow with a team spirit and attitude. I pray for the finances of this company. I pray that the finances will flow. I pray that every debt will be paid in full. I pray for continual favor with every partner that _____ Dance Company does business with. Let your Kingdom Come Your Will Be Done on Earth as you decreed it in heaven over _____ Dance Company. As it is written in heaven, so shall it be on earth. I pray for doors to open in Hollywood, Television and Broadway for _____ Dance Company. I pray that _____ Dance Company will operate in the fullness that you called for them to walk on in this earth.

Reference Scriptures: (Revelation 3:8; Isaiah 50: 7).

Prayer for Tithing on Your Performing Arts Business

A tithe is ten percent of your business earnings. The tithe is God's method to pour out a blessing that you will have not room enough to receive (Malachi 3:10). Therefore, it is a representation that you are in a covenant relationship with him and trust him to provide. Remember that the tithe is a gift and is holy unto the Lord. Therefore, when we spiritually bring our tithe to the Lord, our hearts must be right. If we have ought in our heart against our brother or sister, we must lay our gift at the altar and be reconciled with our brother first and then come offer our gift unto the Lord (Matthew 5:23, 24). We want to make sure that our gift *will be received from God. The tithe was established in the Old Testament and the High Priest received the children of Israel's offering, once a year. So, therefore, we are under the New Testament and Jesus is our High Priest (Hebrews 4:14), and He will receive our tithes and offerings. I believe that you should pray over the tenth of your business earnings with this prayer by faith.*

Father God in Jesus's name, I pray over my tithe and acknowledge that the tithe belongs to you. Lord, your Word says that Abraham gave a tenth of his spoils to Melchizedek (Hebrews 7: 1-10). So, therefore, I come boldly before your throne and bring my tithes and offerings to you. I thank you, Lord, that you have blessed the works of my hands and have given me the power to get wealth (Deuteronomy 8:18). And with this wealth, I am giving you a tenth of my earnings, acknowledging that you have blessed me. I thank you, Lord, that Jesus is the High Priest, and therefore, I bring my gifts to him (Hebrews 4: 14). Lord, your Word says that the tithe is holy unto you (Leviticus 27:30). I, therefore, dedicate a tenth of my earnings to you. I thank you for allowing me to have income from my business. I acknowledge that you have given me this business and the wisdom on how to operate it. I ask that you bless this tithe and offering and multiply it. Even as your Word says, bring all the tithes into the storehouse and prove to you that you will open up the windows of heaven and pour out a blessing that I will have not room enough to receive (Malachi 3: 10). I thank you, Lord, that you are blessing my business above my competitors. So, therefore, I dedicate and consecrate a tenth of my earnings to you. I acknowledge that ten percent of my earnings is a representative that you have given me this business. I thank you, Lord, and I give you the glory and honor and praise in Jesus's Name. Amen.

Reference Scriptures: (Hebrews 7:1-10; Deuteronomy 8:18; Hebrews 4: 14; Leviticus 27:30; Malachi 3:10; Matthew 5:23, 24; Numbers 18: 28).

Prayer for a Building

*The earth is the Lord and the fullness thereof and the inhabitance that dwell therein. The bible says that God knows the secret treasures of dark places, and hidden riches of secret places. He can show you where your building is and the geographical location where it sits. The building may be owned by the bank or by a private party and they may not want that much for it. It is when you pray violet prayers that heaven will move on your behalf. You have to believe nothing is impossible if you have the faith to believe it. If you are trusting in God for a specific building or you have not found a building, this prayer will move the heavens on your behalf **(Please pray the following prayer out loud)**.*

Father your Word says that every place where the soles of _____ (Business name) feet shall tread that

is what you have given unto _____.
So Father, right now in Jesus name, I call forth _____'s building. I speak into the atmosphere a debt free building and that the price will go on sale for _____.
I pray over the address and geographical location that the angels will go before me right now and do battle on _____'s behalf. I bind every spirit that will interfere will the plans of God concerning _____'s building. I loose favor with every title transfer, contract and any other legal documents. I pray over the ground, that the ground of the building is blessed in Jesus name. Lord any un-godly act that has occurred in the building location I cover it with the blood of Jesus. I speak life and prosperity over the address of the building. Now Lord by faith, I receive my building. I thank you that the building will be fix that _____'s will have favor with every contractor, other businesses that we will do business with _____ and the community. I thank you Lord for _____'s building in Jesus name. Amen.

Reference Scriptures: (Psalm 24: 1; Isaiah 45: 3; Joshua 1: 3; Matthew 18: 18).

8

Prayer for a New Building

Father, I thank you, Lord, that we have been faithful over a few things and now you are making us ruler over many. I thank you, Lord, that because we have been faithful that you are enlarging our territory. So, Father, I ask that you lead us to our new location. Let _____ (Business name) administrators be led by your spirit as we scout out our new location. I ask for your divine direction concerning a new building. I thank you in advance for a new business plan as you are enlarging us. I ask that you anoint us for this new move. I ask that we will walk in a new level of anointing and authority for the advancement of your kingdom. I ask that we will bring glory to your name. Now Father God, by faith, we know that your Word framed the heavens. We thank you, Lord, that this new building will be debt-free. Because your Word says that the borrower is servant to the lender. So, Lord, we thank you for a debt-free new location. We thank you, Lord, that this building is dedicated to you. We thank you, Lord, that we will glorify you in this new place in Jesus's name. Amen.

Reference Scriptures: (Proverbs 22:7; Matthew 25:23; Hebrews 11: 3).

Prayer for Choreography

Father God, I give you praise! There is none like you, Oh Lord! You inhabit the praises of your people! Now, Father God, I ask that you stir up the gift of creativity. Move by your spirit Father God, have your way Lord, let your kingdom come your will be done on earth as you have recorded it in heaven. Lord your Word says, "thou shalt also decree a thing, and it shall be established unto thee: and the light shall shine upon thy ways" (Job 22:28). So, Lord, I am decreeing that my gifts in the arts and entertainment industry shall bring and give you praise. Lord your Word also says, "A man's gift maketh room for him, and bringeth him before great men" (Proverbs 18:16). So, Father God, the gifts of the creative arts in dance, theater, and administration will bring me before great men. Also, your Word says, "I beseech you therefore, brethren, by the mercies of God, that ye present your bodies a living sacrifice, holy, acceptable unto God" (Romans 12:1). When the choreography is being creative that you would speak through this gift to give you glory. That heaven will be seen down here on earth to bring you glory. Sanctify every movement, every gesture, Holy Spirit show up in the rehearsal room and have your way. Father God, your word says, "out of your belly shall flow rivers of living water" (John 7:38). So Lord, let your living water flow out of me creating this choreography. Let it be an original to give you glory, honor, and praise. So Lord, right now in Jesus's name, I bind every hindering spirit that would try to come and stop this "piece of movement" to be powerful and effective on stage. I bind every spirit that is NOT of you to try to steal, kill, and destroy the design plan that you want to be established on stage in the name of Jesus. I come against any demonic interruption in the name of Jesus! Lord God, move by your spirit, let your kingdom come your will be done on earth as it is in heaven over this choreography in Jesus's name. Let every dancer, stage manager, and every other staff member function in the capacity that they are called to function in the name of Jesus. I thank you, Lord, for the manifestation in Jesus's name, Amen!

Reference Scriptures: (Proverbs 18:16; Romans 12:1; John 7:38).

10

Prayer for More Students

Father your Word says if I am faithful over a few things you would make me ruler over many things (Matthew 25: 21, 23, KJV). Your Word also says, *"who then is that faithful and wise steward, who his lord shall make ruler over his household, to give them their portion of meat in due season"* (Luke 12:42)? So, Father God, I have been faithful with the students you've entrusted in my hands. I ask that you increase my borders, enlarge my territory (1 Chronicles 4:10), and send more students under my tutelage. I ask that you open doors for me to teach across the United States, Europe, Asia, Africa, Argentina, South America, and any other countries according to your will and plan. I thank you, Lord, for the increase and overflow. I thank you, Lord, that they are coming from the North, South, East, and West. Let your will be done, your kingdom come on earth as you decreed it in heaven (Matthew 6: 10), in Jesus name, AMEN!!!

Reference Scriptures: (Matthew 25: 21, 23; Luke 12:42; 1 Chronicles 4: 10; Matthew 6: 10).

11

Prayer Against Plagiarism and Protecting Your Work

Father God, I thank you, Lord, for a hedge of protection around the borders of my land that includes everything that you have given me to bring glory and honor to your kingdom through ministry and the marketplace. Your Word says, *"He that worketh deceit shall not dwell within my house: he that telleth lies shall not tarry in my sight"* (Psalm 101: 7, KJV). So now, Lord, I bind the spirit of compromise and theft over anyone that would want to compromise their integrity and steal my work(s). I cover every creative idea(s), whether written on paper or through conversation(s) with the Blood of Jesus. Father your Word says, *"He that keepeth his mouth keepeth his life: but he that openeth wide his lips shall have destruction"* (Proverbs 13: 3, KJV). I ask that you put a bridle over my tongue give me wisdom and insight on whom I should share with concerning ideas and projects. Lord, I want you to be able to trust me with the creative ideas that you'd given me. I ask that I would be a good steward over these ideas and that they will become more than ideas but completed projects according to your will and timing. So, therefore, I thank you that ALL creative work(s) and ideas are protected by the Blood of Jesus I decree and declare multi-million-dollar contracts and literary agents to love my work(s). I thank you, Lord, that you have given me wisdom to get every project copy written, trademark to ensure that my _____ name is on each work. I bind every hindering spirit that will try to prolong every work to be officially registered to ensure its natural protection. I lose your favor over every pending project and revised project in Jesus's Name, AMEN!!!

Reference Scriptures: (Psalm 101:7; Proverbs 13:3).

III

Prayers for the Pre-Professional and Non-Professional Dancer

Prayer for a Healthy Diet

Lord God, I come before you in Jesus's name, and I bring my eating habits and diet under your submission. First, I repent for not eating right and slowly destroying my body through unhealthy food choices. I ask that you forgive me, and I forgive myself and realize that today is a new day to do the right thing. I choose to have discipline and a healthy diet so that my body can glorify you. Lord, your word says, "Know ye not that ye are the temple of God, and that the Spirit of God dwelleth in you" (1 Corinthians 3:16)? I want to glorify you through my temple, especially through my food choices. Therefore, I choose to honor God by having a disciplined diet. I choose this because I do not want to give room to the enemy in my diet. Your

Word says, "Brothers, by the mercies of God, to present your bodies as a living sacrifice, holy and acceptable to God, which is your spiritual worship" (Romans 12:1 ESV). I choose today to present my body as a living sacrifice and honor you in what I allow in my temple through my diet. I renounce any seducing spirits of gluttony, peer pressure of eating unhealthily, or any other wrong choices that would destroy my body, such as drugs and alcohol. Father God, I ask that you help me with the right choices concerning my diet so that the right habits will be formed. Lord God, I ask that you bring revelation on what foods to eat that would help me to lose weight in the name of Jesus. Lord, your word says, "I can do all things through Christ which strengtheneth me" (Philippians 4:13 KJV). I thank you, Lord, for giving me the strength to do the right thing concerning my daily diet in Jesus's name, Amen!

Reference Scriptures: (1 Corinthians 3:16; Romans 12:1; Philippians 4:13).

2

Prayer for Spiritual Growth

Your spiritual growth can be accelerated through fasting, prayer, and reading the bible. It is important that when you are a baby Christian that you continually read your bible along with prayer and fasting to break strongholds off your mind and to receive both inner and physical healing. Additionally, revelation knowledge will flow when you fast, pray, and read your bible. This revelation of knowledge will add to your spiritual growth. Praying the Word of God will help you increase your faith, which will help you get spiritually stronger and will aid in your growth.

So, Father God, I come to you in Jesus's name. I ask that you forgive me for any sins that I may have committed knowingly and unknowingly. Father, right now, any spiritual altar that has been made to prevent me from spiritually growing, I command it to be smashed down in Jesus's name. I smash down every altar of prayerlessness, inconsistency, doubt, unbelief, rejection, unworthiness, poor self-esteem, perversion, hatred, un-forgiveness, and any other thing that may exalt itself against the knowledge of God. So now, I replace every ungodly altar that prevented me from growing spiritually with prayer and meditating on the Word of God. I pray Father God, that you will order my steps and that I will know and hear your voice and the voice of a stranger I will not follow. I pray that you will continually increase my discernment, and I will see the traps and snares of the enemy. I pray that I will be rooted in grounded in your Word that I will have the full revelation knowledge of your love that surpasses all understanding. That nothing can separate me from your love. I pray for your resurrection power to make every dead place in my life to come alive again. I thank you, Lord, that you are Jehovah Rapha, the God that heals me. I thank you for my supernatural breakthrough in Jesus's name. Amen.

Reference Scriptures: (Daniel 1: 17, 20; 2 Peter 3: 18; 2 Thessalonians 1: 3, Ephesians 3: 17-21; Psalms 37:23).

Prayer Against the Spirit of Fear

Moving in God's timing in your purpose requires your faith, which means the enemy will attack you with the spirit of fear. The spirit of fear will paralyze you from walking into your divine purpose. We have to guard our hearts and mind against the spirit of fear. The bible says that God has not given you the spirit of fear but of power, love, and of a sound mind (2 Timothy 1:7). Fear and faith cannot exist together. Therefore, we want to operate in the spirit of faith. When God wants to bring you into a "new place," you have to attack the spirit of fear off your mind. It would be beneficial if you can pray in tongues before you pray this. Let us pray to break every stronghold of fear.

Father God, right now in Jesus's name, I attack the spirit of fear at its root. Every negative circumstance that the enemy used, I cancel every assignment of fear off my life. God your Word says that now faith is the substance of things hoped for and the evidence of things not seen. I thank you, Lord, that I will walk in faith not in fear, in Jesus Name. Amen

Reference Scriptures: (Hebrews 11:1; 2 Timothy 1:7).

Prayer For Your Teacher

The bible says that we should pray for those in authority. 1 Timothy 2:1 & 2 says, "I exhort therefore, that, first of all, supplications, prayers, intercessions, and giving of thanks, be made for all men; for kings, and for all that are in authority; that we may lead a quiet and peaceable life in all godliness and honesty" (KJV). It is our responsibility to pray for those in leadership that they will make the right, fair, and just decisions and that they will not be influenced by ungodly counsel. We have to pray that the spirit of God will lead them in their decision-making.

Father God, you said in your word to pray for our leaders, so Lord, right now in Jesus's name, I pray for my dance teacher(s). I pray that every decision that they make with rehearsals, performances, who they trust in authoritative positions in their company and outside vendors that they will be led by your spirit and not of the flesh. Father God, your Word says cursed is the man that put his trust in the arm of flesh but blessed is the man that trust in the Lord and who hopes in him. So, Father God, right now in Jesus's name, I bind the spirit of manipulation and control over their thoughts, over their mind, over their decision-making process, and every other thing that is not of you. Lord, I thank you that my teacher _____ will trust in you and that your Word will be the final authority in their life. I thank you, Lord, that you put them in this leadership position and that they will be led by your spirit and not of their flesh. I thank you, Lord, for the victory concerning them in Jesus's name. Amen

Reference Scriptures: (1 Timothy 2:1, 2; Jeremiah 17: 5, 7).

5

Prayer For Your Dance Team

The enemy will always try to bring division, strife, envy, and jealousy to any team whose mission is to glorify Christ. I am encouraging you to pick up the mantle of prayer to pray for the leaders and team members. The enemy knows the call of God on the vision of your dance team, and he will try to disrupt and dismantle it.

Father, I come before you right now in Jesus's name. I ask you to forgive us for our sins that we have committed knowingly and unknowingly. Lord, I uplift _____ Dance Team and I cover them with the Blood of Jesus. Father, your word says, "Behold, how good and how pleasant it is for brethren to dwell together in unity! It is like precious ointment upon the head, that ran down upon the beard, even Aaron's beard: that went down to the skirts of his garments" (Psalm 133: 2, 3). So Father, right now in Jesus's name, I bind the spirit of strife, contention, discord, envy, and jealousy! Have your way, Lord Father, I ask that you do a shift in the thinking of the minds of the dance team members. Father your Word says, "that their hearts might be comforted, being knit together in love, and unto all riches of the full assurance of understanding, to the acknowledgment of the mystery of God, and of the Father, and of Christ" (Colossians 2:2). Lord, I ask that you will knit our hearts together in love and that we will be able to minister to each other and your people. Father, I decree that _____ Dance Team will be filled with the knowledge of your will in all wisdom and spiritual understanding; that _____ Dance Team will walk worthy of the Lord unto all pleasing, being fruitful in every good work, and increasing in the knowledge of God (Colossians 1:9b, 10). I decree that the fruit will remain in their hearts and lives today in Jesus's Name, Amen!

Reference Scriptures: (Psalm 133: 2, 3; Colossians 2:2; Colossians 1:9b, 10).

IV

Prayers for Deliverance

1

Prayers Against the Spirit of Perversion

If you have sexual-sin or any other type of perversion running rampant in your ministry, it will affect the anointing from flowing and coming forth. You do not want to make strange sacrifices unto the Lord or offer up a strange fire. This could affect your ministry where God wants to take it and ultimately destroy your ministry. Therefore, you must remove sin from your ministry. If you know of a dancer that is struggling with the spirit of perversion, it is wise that they would go through deliverance and spend some time fasting and praying. According to Vine's Complete Expository Dictionary, the word perversion is derived from perverse or pervert, which means in Greek metastrepho, "to transform into something of an opposite character" (meta, signifying *"a change," and strepho,) as the Judaizers sought to "pervert the gospel of Christ." As a leader, you want to guard against this wicked spirit coming into your ministry. It is your responsibility that when you go forth and minister as a group that you are not releasing a spirit of perversion or lust unto the congregation. The bible says, let's come before the Lord with clean hands and a pure heart. Additionally, you want to make sure that you are operating with clean hands and a pure heart. Remember, what comes from the head flows down to the body. You want to make sure that as Christ put you as the head of the ministry that you are walking in integrity and not a perverse spirit **(Please pray the following prayer below out loud).***

Heavenly Father, I come before you in Jesus's name, and I ask that you forgive me from walking in the spirit of perversion. I ask that you forgive me for opening the door to the spirit of perversion, lust, fornication, adultery, homosexuality, or bestiality. Father God, I renounce _____ along with the act and the spirits that are operating behind the act. Your Word says if my people, which are called by my name, shall humble themselves and pray, and seek my face, and turn from their wicked ways; then I will hear from heaven and will forgive their sins and heal their land. I ask you, Lord, to heal and deliver me. Anything that is foundationally connected to the spirit of perversion from my bloodline, both father's and mother's side; I renounce it and close the door. Any type of perversion that was passed to me through molestation, I ask that you uproot it out of my foundational core and sever any soul tie between the molester and myself. Any type of molestation that I may have done to someone, I ask that you forgive me, and I break every spirit of perversion that I passed to the person. I ask that you will deliver and set them free. I break every soul-tie with any sexual partners right now in Jesus's name. I ask that you wash me with your son's blood. Create in me a clean heart, Lord, and renew a right spirit within me. Father God, repentance means to completely turn away from my sin and do not go back. So, Lord, I thank you for a heart of repentance, and now I completely turn away from my sin.

Now, Lord, I understand that your living Word is the final authority in my life, even though the world may deem these things as right. Help me to stay away from anyone that is actively participating in these sins. Help me to pray for those that are struggling in these areas. Father God, we know that your love covers a multitude of sins, and hatred stirs up strife. So Lord, now that you have delivered me, let me not be judgmental on anyone's struggle. Help me to love them unconditionally and pray for them daily. I ask that you will help me keep my focus and God-given purpose. Help me to walk in my anointing and authority that you have placed in me. I thank you, Lord, for delivering those that I have associated with. I thank you, Lord, that your Word is the final authority in my life and forevermore in Jesus's name. Amen.

Reference Scriptures: (2 Chronicles 7:14; Psalm 51: 2, 10; 1 Peter 4:8).

2

Removing Every Altar of Idolatry

Remember, the enemy was the archangel for worship. He was created by God to be head of worship in heaven. The bible tells us that Lucifer had beautiful gems and stones and horns in him. When he physically moved, he made a beautiful melody. Ezekiel 28: 13-17 reads:

Thou hast been in Eden the garden of God; every precious stone was thy covering, the sardius, topaz, and the diamond, the beryl, the onyx, and the jasper, the sapphire, the emerald, and the carbuncle, and gold: the workmanship of thy tabrets and of thy pipes was prepared in thee in the day that thou wast created. Thou art the anointed cherub that covereth; and I have set thee so: thou wast upon the holy mountain of God; thou hast walked up and down in the midst of the stones of fire. Thou wast perfect in thy ways from the day that thou wast created, till iniquity was found in thee. By the multitude of thy merchandise, they have filled the midst of thee with violence, and thou hast sinned: therefore I will cast thee as profane out of the mountain of God: and I will destroy thee, O covering cherub, from the midst of the stones of fire. Thine heart was lifted up because of thy beauty, thou hast corrupted thy wisdom by reason of thy brightness: I will cast thee to the ground, I will lay thee before kings, that they may behold thee.

Lucifer was filled with pride. In Isaiah 14: 12-14 it reads, *"How art thou fallen from heaven, O Lucifer, son of the morning! How art thou cut down to the ground, which didst weaken the nations! For thou hast said in thine heart, I will ascend into heaven, I will exalt my throne above the stars of God: I will sit also upon the mount of the congregation, in the sides of the north: I will ascend above the heights of the clouds: I will be like the most High."* He saw the angels worshiping God and desired to take God's place. When Lucifer was kicked out of heaven, we were then created to worship God in his stead. The enemy hates the fact that you were created to take his place. He wants your worship toward the Lord to be contaminated. Anything that you do for the Lord, the devil wants it to be perverted. As a believer and a worshiper of God, you have to continually seek the Lord to make sure that we put nothing before Him. The Lord comes first in our lives. When we worship the Lord, we should have clean hands and a pure heart. We want to live a consecrated and sanctified life unto the Lord. We are vessels for the Lord to use. Remember, everything you do is as if it is worship unto the Lord.

Therefore, it is up to you to guard your heart and remove any stumbling block that would hinder you from operating in the glory of God and walking in the fullness of His spirit. The bible says to *"keep thy heart with all diligence; for out of it are the issues of life"* (Proverbs 4: 23). Additionally, the bible also says that *"God is a Spirit: and they that worship him must worship him in spirit and in truth"* (John 4:24). Remember, it is a spiritual heart condition. Whatever flows out of our spirit is a representation of what's in our hearts. We must be proactive and make sure that there is no hindrance for the glory of God to operate in our lives.

With this being said, the Holy Spirit will bring to your attention the hindrances of any spiritual altars that were made by you or through your ancestral bloodline. Also, any covenants that you or your ancestors made with false-gods, these altars, and graven images MUST be torn down. *(Exodus 34:13; Deuteronomy 7:5; Deuteronomy 12: 3)*. How do you tear them down? You tear them down through prayer. *Please note: If you made a natural altar, you should burn any object and dispose of the altar and renounce all articles that are on the altar.*

Note: Please pray this prayer out loud and verbally renounce every altar.

So Father, right now in Jesus's name, I stand in the gap for my ancestors that had made altars of idolatry (both on my father's and mother's side). I pray that every altar that was made through ignorance or through following family tradition, I repent on their behalf right now in Jesus name. So Lord, right now in Jesus's name, I renounce the altar of _____ that was made through my father and mother's side right now in Jesus's name. I renounce the spirits that are associated with these altars and close the door to them right now in Jesus's name. I renounce every un-godly altar that I made such as _____ and I close the door to these altars right now in Jesus's name. I renounce every spirit associated with any altar that was created by me right now in Jesus's name. Any seeds that bore fruit through the altars and false gods, I command it to wither up and die right now in Jesus's name (Matthew 21: 20)! I ask you to cleanse me from any defilement right now (Psalm 51). So Father, I publicly announce that I create an altar of worship unto you. I decree and declare that I shall be on fire for God! I decree and declare that no weapon form against me shall prosper (Isaiah 54:17). I thank you, Lord, that I am covered under the Blood of Jesus Christ; my ancestors are covered under the Blood of Jesus Christ. I thank you, Lord, that all my ancestors shall know the Lord and be on fire for God! I thank you, Lord, for the manifestation of this prayer in Jesus's name, AMEN!!!

Reference Scriptures: (Psalms 24:4; Ezekiel 28:
14-17; Isaiah 14: 12-14;
Proverbs 4:23; John 4: 24;
Exodus 34: 13; Deuteronomy 7:5;
Deuteronomy 12: 3; Matthew 21: 20;
Psalm 51; Isaiah 54: 17).

A Prayer for Your Star to Rise and Bless The Nations

Father, in the name of Jesus, I come before you, asking you to forgive me for any sins that I committed knowingly and unknowingly. Lord, your Word says, if I confess my sins that you are just and to cleanse me from all unrighteousness. So Father God, right now in Jesus's name, I ask that you forgive me from _____.
I ask that you wash me whiter than snow and create in me a clean heart and renew a right spirit within me. Now, Lord, I asked that you prosper me and make my name great. Lord, your Word says in Genesis 12:2, "I will make of thee a great nation, and I will bless thee, and make thy name great, and thou shat be a blessing" (KJV). Father, I ask that you will make my name great so that I may be a

blessing to many. Lord, I dedicate every gift, talent, and ability to you. I ask that I will please you and that I will bring you glory and that my light will shine before many. I ask that you will increase my borders from the North, South, East, and West and that my gifts will bring me before great men and women. Now, Lord, I dispatch my angels to go forth now to do the necessary work on my behalf, in Jesus's name. Amen!

Final Thoughts

God desires to bless you and prosper His children. The bible says, "Beloved I wish above all things that thou mayest prosper and be in health even as thy soul prospereth" (Jeremiah 29:11, KJV).

Go forth and do what God has called you to do.

Author Contact Details

Email:
swhittentheatricals@gmail.com
or prayingforthearts@yahoo.com

Website
www.swazettewhitten.com

Other books by Swazette Whitten

30 Days of Prayers:
Praying for Your Future King

www.ingramcontent.com/pod-product-compliance
Lightning Source LLC
LaVergne TN
LVHW041632070426
835507LV00008B/577